SOUTH SHIELDS
PUBS

SOUTH SHIELDS PUBS

EILEEN BURNETT

AMBERLEY PUBLISHING

First published 2014

Amberley Publishing
The Hill, Stroud
Gloucestershire, GL5 4EP

www.amberley-books.com

Copyright © Eileen Burnett, 2014

The right of Eileen Burnett to be identified as the
Author of this work has been asserted in
accordance with the Copyrights, Designs and
Patents Act 1988.

ISBN 978 1 4456 4200 0 (print)
ISBN 978 1 4456 4208 6 (e-book)

British Library Cataloguing in Publication Data.
A catalogue record for this book is available from
the British Library.

Typesetting by Amberley Publishing.
Printed in the UK.

Introduction

In 1821, only fifty hotels, inns and taverns were mentioned in Kelly's Directory, although there were a lot more. In a note in the vestry book of 1796, it states there were 164; magistrates were requested to refuse licences to all publicans not paying the poor rate. By 1827, 153 landlords advertised their establishments. My three-times-great-grandfather Stephen Falp had the Shakespeare Inn at Comical Corner in 1859 and my husband's four-times-great-grandfather, Benjamin Golightley, had the Hope and Anchor in Wapping Street, which he changed to the Hope in 1828. Unfortunately, most of the hotels, inns and taverns were pulled down before photography became popular.

This book is about the old hotels, inns and taverns of South Shields, Westoe, and Harton. They were situated mostly along the riverside, from Slake Terrace, Temple Town and Corstorphine Town, to the west, West and East Holborn, the Mill Dam and the Market Place. The old streets along the riverside were Thrift Street, Long Row, Wapping Street, Shadwell Street and Pilot Street, to the mouth of the Tyne. We then turn south to 'the Lawe' and back to the Market Place, not forgetting Union Alley. Then we go down King Street, along Ocean Road to the old workhouse on what was German Street, along the streets behind Ocean Road and again to Commercial Road, Laygate, Westoe, Harton and back to Slack Terrace.

Many streets do not exist anymore. Few of the old hotels, inns and taverns have survived. The Tyne Dock Hotel (Kennedy's), the Rose & Crown, the Earl Gray, Adam and Eve, the Pier, the Royal Hotel, The Stag's Head, Lambton Arms and the Mechanics are but a few.

In 1871, James Snell advertised the Alexander Hotel, which stood at the far side of what was the Tyne Dock Arches at the junction of the Jarrow Road and Leam Lane, now Newcastle Road. Made famous by Catherine Cookson as the tavern where she was sent on occasion for a jug of beer, it was more popularly known by the dock and railway workers as the '27', owing to the number of Staiths (twenty-six altogether) that used to be at Tyne Dock. It has been known as the '27' ever since.

Travelling from the south we would have come along the Chester-le-Street Toll Road towards Temple Town. This ancient road had at one time skirted that great expanse of muddy water of the Slake, which at high tide could have been quite daunting. The Slake was partly reclaimed to build docks, and Slake Terrace came into being in the 1840s. Slake Terrace became known for its many drinking establishments.

The Grapes Hotel started life as the Dock House Inn, advertised in 1856 by Thomas Blench, who changed its name to the Grapes Hotel in 1865. This photograph from 1904 shows just how magnificent this would have looked to a weary traveller or sailor when it was first built. Stephen Sheriff bought the Grapes Hotel for £13,725 when it was auctioned by the executors of Thomas Blench in 1901. The Grapes Hotel lost its licence and closed on 5 February 1960.

The Banks of the Tyne was built in 1848 as a beer house. James Nichol, its first landlord, was also a tailor. In 1853, Thomas Newton became landlord, but it was not advertised again until 1865, when James Conway was the landlord. The Banks of the Tyne closed on 8 January 1959.

On the far right was the North Eastern Hotel, which was another most impressive building, originally built as the Dock Hotel. Planning permission was granted on 21 November 1855 to Miss A. M. Wood to build the 'Dock Hotel'; in 1860, it became the North Eastern when James Thomas Southerland became landlord. When sold by Messrs Vasey & Reed in 1891, Robert Henderson bought it for £8,570, a considerable sum of money in those days. On 2 October 1958 it closed and the licence was transferred to the Lord Clyde.

William Davidson opened the Engineers Arms in 1883 and by 1890 had extended the premises, calling the new hotel the Empress. Many people will remember the Empress Hotel by its nickname of 'Lowery's'. Daniel Vinton Lowery was the licensee from June 1932 until the 1950s. Like most of the buildings in Slake Terrace, the Empress closed on 31 January 1960.

The first tavern to be seen looking south from the Slake was the Rose & Crown in Dean Lane. This pretty little cottage belonged to John Gray, who was also a market gardener. In 1834, he changed the name to the Dean Mouth, as it was situated beside the Dean Burn. The Dean Burn Inn, as it was later to be called, stayed in the Gray Family until Mrs Gray died in the 1860s. It stood opposite St Mary's church until it was pulled down in the early 1900s.

In 1808, Simon Temple leased the coal royalties from the Dean and Chapter of Durham and sunk the pit shaft that was to be better known as Temple Town Pit. Today, Temple Town has been swallowed up into Commercial Road and, apart from the sign on the side of Kennedy's, little remains of this once vibrant area.

Travelling east from Jarrow, the Plough Inn, built in 1809, was the first tavern travellers would have seen on their way towards South Shields before the building of Slake Terrace. Its landlord, Thomas Harrison, had the tavern until around 1840, when Thomas Turner took it over and changed the name to the Tyne Dock Hotel. On 4 December 1890, R. S. & D. Crosthwaite were granted planning permission to rebuild the Tyne Dock Hotel and it is from this building we get the date of 1809. When John Kennedy had the hotel, he used to have a bottle that was specially made with his name and the hotel name on it. The name of the Tyne Dock Hotel, which was thirteen letters, and the two spaces between, with the space at the bottom, gave the bottle a measurement of 16 fluid ounces, or 1 pint, for people coming into the jug and bottle for their spirits. Over the last century, the inside has been refurbished a number of times due to the flooding of the area, but it has managed to keep the old world décor. Annette, the barmaid with whom I spoke, told me that Carl the manager has been there for nineteen years.

The Tyne Dock Hotel as it is today has had its name changed to 'Kennedy's', and once again, just as it was over 200 years ago, it is the first public house you see on your way into South Shields.

Corstorphine Town, dated much later than Temple Town, was named after Robert Corstorphine. He had planned to build a Commercial Centre at the west side of the town. This area became known as 'New Market'.

This very impressive hotel stood facing Temple Town to greet commercial travellers, hopeful that they would stop to rest after a long journey. It boasted a lounge bar of 42 feet, a snug, a large tap room, a kitchen and a scullery on the ground floor, a first-floor billiard room, eight bedrooms and a bathroom with hot and cold water on the second floor when it was sold in 1875 for £6,600. The landlord at the time was J. Emmerson. The London Hotel had its licence refused on 5 February 1919, and the land was incorporated into Readhead's Shipyards.

Cookson's Arms is on the far right, looking toward the 'New Market Clock' and Commercial Road. The Cookson's Arms was owned by Robert Corstorphine from when it was first built until the early 1870s, when William Elisha Bennett became its landlord. The Cookson Arms served the community and visitors alike up until the early 1960s. It was a well-frequented watering hole for the many shipyard and office workers from nearby. Many people today still have fond memories of the Cookson's Arms, which was demolished; its licence was transferred to the White Horse, Quarry Lane.

The Burton Cellars is the small building between the Methodist church and the Neptune Inn. In 1900, the landlord was James Routledge; on 31 May 1904, it surrendered its licence and closed.

The Neptune Inn, which is to the right of the photograph, was built in the middle part of the 1800s. Like most of the inns in Corstorphine Town, it was owned by Swinburne & Company, Brewers, Spring Lane. Like the Burton Cellars, the Neptune became a victim of the expansion of the shipyards.

At the junction of Corstorphine Town and West Holborn was the Dock House at High Dock. The Dock House was owned by John Miller in 1789. Hugh Rodham changed its name several times; it was sometimes the Dock and Yard, then the Ship in Dock. In 1850, when the tavern was taken over by Robert Miller, it became the Dock House, then changed to the West Dock Inn in 1854 and back to the Dock Yard by 1856, keeping that name until 1865, when once again it changed to Dock House. In 1866, however, Robert Miller once again changed the name to West Dock Inn, keeping that name until it closed. According to Hodgson, the pub retained its licence long after it had ceased to make use of it and had been enclosed within the limits of the shipyard. This building is still at the end of what was Corstorphine Town within McNulty's Yard. Could this be the Dock House that Hugh Rodham had?

West Holborn, a much older part of the town, no longer exists as such. The only memories come from an older generation, who tell of the riverside where the shipyards and manufacturing industries once stood.

The Commercial Hotel was first advertised in 1828 by John Brock as the Commercial Tavern. In August 1880, fire broke out in the hotel, which quickly spread, and the building, along with the stock in trade, was destroyed. Luckily, no one was injured. William Sproat was insured and he had the hotel rebuilt in 1881. The Commercial Hotel stood outside the West Dock entrance of Readhead's Shipyards and was a well-established watering hole for many a shipyard worker. It was a unique survivor of a Victorian dockside tavern, and had a Victorian Lady as a ghost, which one landlady named Victoria; many of the later regulars might remember her. Dave and Pat McGregor took over the Commercial Hotel in 1982 and would have seen many changes, with the decline of the shipyards and lunchtime drinking becoming a thing of the past. Unfortunately, in March 2008, the last pints were pulled and in February 2013 the council had it pulled down.

The Middle Dock Hotel started life as the Cross Keys, at the corner of the Point Ferry Landing near the Penny Pie Stairs. It was built in the early 1800s. In 1857, John Wardle had it rebuilt and it became a well-established meeting place, as can be seen here, for workers from the nearby shipyards. When this photograph was taken, Sarah Lawson Cockburn was the landlady. It unfortunately closed in the late 1930s.

Like West Holborn, East Holborn was an older part of the town and, as the town expanded, the Holborns became a warren of streets and alleyways with hotels, taverns and inns all vying for passing trade.

The Cumberland Arms was on the corner of Hill Street and East Holborn. Built in the early 1800s, John Nelson was the licensee in 1821. In 1894, under the ownership of Bell & Taylor, it became known as the Cumberland Grill Inn. Daniel O'Conner was the last licensee in the 1960s.

The Rose & Crown was originally built in the late 1700s to early 1800s, Anthony Gray being the landlord in 1827. It has been rebuilt several times over the years for the widening of the road. In 1903 Stephen Sheriff sold the land upon which the original hotel was built and submitted plans for a new public house to be built on the corner of Carpenter Street. In the 1950s, the Rose & Crown was once again altered, but of all the licenced houses that once graced Holborn, it is the only one that remains. During recent times it has seen celebrities such as Terry McDermott, the footballer, and Jarrow singer John Miles among its patrons and *George Gently* has been filmed both inside and outside the pub.

One of the more unusually-named public houses, the Hop Pole, was one of the largest pubs on the riverside. An 1824 poster gives the address as a little above the Mill Dam. It was said to be haunted by a 'Red Lady' chanting strange songs in the late 1700s. A piece in the *Gazette* on 15 November 1940, just after it had been pulled down, said this about it all:

She was no ordinary lady of the spectral world, for she was richly attired in robes of red, chanting weird songs stalking the back chamber of the house with heavy foot, and was sometimes accompanied by transparent flames and the noise of clanking chains, altogether an unpleasant person.

The vicar of the local church – the Rev. John Hack was called in to perform the act of exorcism - at first he declined but then a date was set and with much pomp – and the choir chanting the Laudamus, sailors and their wives, beer woman and chandlers and carpenters, with a good number of sail makers and panners, which made much din and drowned out the holy music. When he came to the chamber looking out upon the river the Red Lady appeared. It was a gruesome room. The door, which he left open that he might the more easily retreat, closed, and a great flame proceeded out of the earth so that a light dazzled him and the smoke choked him and he was much afreared. He cried aloud for succour but none could get into the room which was securely bolted and held by the ghostly hands. At length the door flew open and a horrible sight the people saw. In the centre of the room stood the Red Lady with the clergyman clasped tightly in her arms. Sulphur made the air hot and stifling and it seemed the man was in a faint from fright or fumes. The room was splashed with red streaks as with blood and flames rose hither and thither from the floor. Yet nothing burned. As the people ran to rescue the minister the lady slowly faded from their gaze and when they came to the centre of the apartment it was tenantless. Both minister and spirit had disappeared in the earth. But next morning Mr Hack crept up to his own door, bedraggled and bruised and wet. His gown and hair were singed, yet it appeared he had suffered more from the water than the fire. Never a word said he concerning his sojourn through the night, but he called lustily for strong waters so the good Mrs Stillroom, his housekeeper, made no doubt his undoing. He drained the horn in one gulp, betook himself to his bed and slept for twenty and four hours. Then returned to his holy duties with exceeding zeal and many marvelled at his ministrations, for they made no doubt he was possessed. Although the reverend gentleman kept a stoic silence on the matter, so far as his parishioners were concerned, his explanation and his influence were not withheld in other quarters, because as a result of his efforts the Preventive was greatly strengthened at Shields. Then following the denouement. One morning a strange craft, laden with silks and rich brandies from France, fell into the hands of the King's Men on the spot. They found a secret passage under the wharf to great vaults below the haunted chamber. A trap door led to the room above and there they found the red robes of the apparition, the clanking chains and a keg of red paint.

The 'free traders' got clean away and with them, too, went the mistress of the house and with her maids.

The Hop Pole closed in February 1937.

The Alnwick Castle was situated near the Mill Dam, with the 'old' Commercial Road to the right. Its address was originally Brewery Lane in 1821, when Choice (sic) Smallman was the owner. The address stayed as Brewery Lane until 1844, when it became East Holborn. This hotel also had a lion above the door. Having a straight tail, this lion was possibly to reflect the hotel's association with Alnwick and the Percy Lion. The lion was once described as having a tail straight out like a pump handle.

The Cumberland Arms, in the centre, started as the Ship in the 1700s but was changed to the Ship Aurora in the early 1800s by Sarah Weatherburn. In 1834, it was called the Mill Dam House; it would have been situated on the bank of the Mill Dam. In 1853, Thomas Smart renamed the tavern the Cumberland Arms.

Situated as it was between East Holborn to the left, with Commercial Road far left and Brewery Lane to the right, the Mill Dam on the far right and facing Coronation Street, it became a place for seamen to meet. During the 1930s depression, when there was a problem with the seaman, it had already been taken over by Mrs Hamid, an Egyptian lady, as a boarding house.

The Locomotive was first advertised by Emanuel Hayton in 1850, although it is thought to be older. It was possibly named the Locomotive because at the time there used to be a passenger railway station at the end of the alleyway to the right. It has been said that it was supposedly used by the press gangs to crew the many ships that once docked at the Mill Dam Quay.

In 1899, the Durham and Northumberland Licence Victualier Syndicate Limited became the owners, keeping the Locomotive for many years. According to some, the Locomotive had its share of ghosts; a retired seaman, who was a regular in the pub – which in those days was 'beer only' – had a reputation as a hard drinker and quite a loud talker. This gentleman would brag of his exploits to all and sundry, becoming quite terse if he thought that those listening were not taking him seriously. One night, after drinking a quantity of ale, he staggered to the top of the cellar stairs, swayed and, after muttering, fell headlong down to his death. A week went by and all had been quiet, then someone saw the old sailor walking past the door. He was apparently seen right up until the 1950s.

In October 1990, the locomotive won the Pub of the Year. In 2011, the Steamboat was the CAMRA (Campaign for Real Ale) pub of the year for the third year in a row. The pub is full of character and atmosphere with friendly staff; it has a raised seating area within the bar and a small lounge. With eight hand pulls, it offers an impressive range of beers from independent breweries and microbreweries, plus a real cider.

This very impressive building started as the Brighton Beach in the early 1800s. In 1821, George Marchbank gave the address as East Holborn, but in 1827, the address became Coronation Street. In 1844, John Potts renamed it the Railway Inn, the railway station being behind the inn at the time. This beautifully rebuilt public house has been haunted by phantoms of the past. A landlady, possibly Mrs Margaret Simm (1856–65), who had taken over the inn after many years in the Merchant Tailors Arms in Ferry Street, made it her home. She refused to retire, despite her failing health, and died there. Before long, it seems, drinkers saw her back behind the bar.

Built as the Waterloo Tavern, Jane Dixon first advertised this pub in 1834. Taken over in 1883 as the Hilda Arms, it stood at the corner of St Hilda's Lane and Coronation Street, the first landlord being Charles Fairington. When it closed in August 1929, compensation was paid to the owner and on 10 February 1938 the licence was transferred to the Simonside Arms, Newcastle Road.

This was originally called the Ferry Boat Hotel, Alum House Ham, when John Middleton was the landlord in 1827. In 1855, Emily Snowdon renamed it the Steam Ferry Hotel. In the mid-1860s, it was the Ferry Hotel, Ferry Street. Said to be a relic of the Cooksons' old home, it also functioned as an auxiliary Customs House at one time before the new one we know today was built.

The inside of the Ferry Hotel, which kept its old world look; gin was still sold from barrels and the Guinness, Extra Stout, which was quite a common drink in the 1950s, was on draught at what looks to be 2s (10 new pence) per glass. By the 1960s, the Ferry Hotel had become quite notorious for being a house of disrepute; foreign sailors from all over the world, coming into the ports on the river, would come to drink and the young girls would meet them for a night out. By 1991, it was known for its strippers and, in November, the landlady Helen Gibson and her husband, Arthur, had tried to recruit local talent but ended up recruiting them from Newcastle's Uptown Glamour Agency. It was closed in March 1999.

This building, dating back to the early 1700s, was owned by Ralph Carr Esq. in the 1760s. The Alum House Tavern was first mentioned in the Courant in January 1839, when Mr Jackson was licensee. In September 1839, owners Kirkley, Swinburne and Company, of the Market Brewery, advertised the inn to let. In August 1840, the Alum House was once again up to let. Mr John Hart the landlord does not seem to have kept the place long. Swinburne and Co. had their own brand of whisky, 'ROL', which stood for Rare Old Liquor.

In a book by Mike Hallowell, I read that the Alum House has had many ghosts; a 'Grey Lady', who apparently was known to frequent the toilets, a giggling Irish prostitute and a Victorian gentleman are but a few of many.

During the Second World War, the Alum House was used to house the Home Guard of the Durham Light Infantry, whose crest could be seen above an upstairs fireplace.

The Alum House has not always been a public house; over the last century it has been owned by the Tyne Dock Engineering Company as offices. In 1982, it was opened as the Contract Furnishing Co., owned by Mr David Donnelly. The premises were a retail showroom, offices and a workshop; a new shop-front was also installed.

In 1991, a fire jeopardised the sale of the Alum House, but today it is once more looking more like its former self.

Dean Street was quite a broad thoroughfare leading down to the ferry landing from the Market Place. The Nunnerie, built in the late 1800s, had only a small door next to Mather & Co. Wine and Spirit Merchants as an entrance in Dean Street. The main part of the public house was at the back of Dean Street, where the entrance was more frequently used. The Nunnerie was once owned by the Douthwaite Spencer family until 1935, when Lorimer & Clark Limited took it over. It was then pulled down for the regeneration of the Market area.

Situated at the junction of Ferry Street and West Street, the Willie Wouldhave started life as the Spirit Vaults in 1865; it was owned by William Snaith Reay and became known as Reay's Vaults. William Yates took over the Vaults in 1886 and it became the Willie Wouldhave. It was more popularly known as the Boiled Oil by many of its clientele because, I have been told by Mrs Bates, of the strong ale that was served. The patrons were only allowed two pints and no more in any one day because of its strength. I am sure there are other stories about the name. A portrait of William Wouldhave, taken from the public house, was to be preserved in South Shields Library, now the museum, when the pub was demolished in 1967.

An engraving by A. Reid of the Market Place and the Old Town Hall around 1850, looking north towards Thrift Street and the windmill on Harding's Hill.

The Market Hotel was originally called the Albion Hotel when Isabella Clark was landlady in 1839; Isabella was also landlady of the Waterloo Inn at the same time, whether part of the same public house I do not know. In 1867, William English, a sadler in Dean Street, changed the name to the Market Hotel.

The Norfolk & Suffolk was originally called the King's Head in 1821, when Thomas Robson was the landlord. In 1834, William Guy Vennell became landlord and in 1839 he changed the name to the Norfolk & Suffolk. The last landlord of the Norfolk & Suffolk was John Hart Simpson, who took over as licensee in April 1955.

Both public houses were pulled down for the regeneration of the Market Place.

The Three Indian Kings stood in the north-west corner of the Market Place, where the Commando recently stood. The Three Indian Kings was built in the 1700s, a name which it kept until the early 1890s, when James McCulloch was the licensee. By 1898, the Three Indian Kings had been taken over by R. A. Osborne as the dining rooms.

The Exchange Vaults, which stood in the north-west corner of the Market Place, was first advertised by Joseph Anderson in 1879. In later years it became quite a haunt for the shipyard workers from nearby and it was close to Cowie's Ship store building. Damaged during the war, the Exchange Vaults managed to survive until 1957, when its licence was transferred to the Pickwick Arms.

The Locomotive Inn *(far left)*, on the corner of Thrift Street and the Market Place, was originally called the Market Place Tavern in 1833, when the landlord was William Cook. In 1846, John Brunton changed the name to the Hat & Feathers Inn. In 1881, James Harrington renamed the public house the Locomotive Inn, the name it kept until it lost its licence in March 1937. Like many of the buildings in the market, it was badly damaged in October 1941. On 11 August 1955, the licence was transferred to the Jolly Stewart, Stewart Crescent, Marsden.

The City of Durham was originally called the Durham Arms Inn in 1827, when Margaret Cairns was landlady. In 1864, when Samuel Brown when become the landlord, he changed the name to the City of Durham Hotel.

The Highlander stood next to the City of Durham from as early as 1821, when it was first advertised by Andrew Jameson. James Scott became the landlord in 1859 and changed the name to the Old Highlander. When Samuel Brown became the landlord in 1871, he incorporated it into the City of Durham.

Rebuilt in 1937 after it was demolished to make way for the new road, River Drive, it was demolished by enemy bombing in 1941 and rebuilt in 1947, only to be demolished again in 1960

The Rose & Crown had been in the Market Place from 1765, standing on the opposite corner of Union Alley to the City of Durham. In 1774, Robert Feard was the landlord and in 1782 Henry Baker took over the inn. John Anderson took over the inn on the death of Henry Baker and advertised it as 'fitted up in such a manner, as, he trusts, will afford the most satisfactory accommodation to those who please to favour him with their support, which it shall be his particular attention to merit. Post Chaises, able horses, and careful drivers, good stabling and Coach-houses'. In 1827, when James Young was landlord, the Rose & Crown was also the Excise Office and one of the town's coaching inns. Like the Three Indian Kings, which had faced the Rose & Crown for over 100 years, it also was taken over in 1898 and became the dining rooms of J. Petrolino.

The Mariner's Arms was another Georgian public house that had stood in the Market Place since 1827, George Harrison being the landlord. By 1834, Frances Harrison had taken over the running of the public house, where she stayed until 1855. Although most of the Market Place was damaged by enemy bombing in 1941, the Mariner's Arms survived until August 1954, when its licence was transferred to the Queen's Head, Claypath Lane.

The Grapes Hotel, which was next to the Tram Hotel, started as the Commercial Hotel in 1844, when Thomas Hopper was the landlord. In 1854, William Medcalf had the name changed to the Turf Tavern, but when John Parker became the landlord in 1856, he changed the name to the Grapes Hotel. The Grapes Hotel was unfortunately another casualty of the enemy bombing in 1941.

The Tram Hotel was called the Cross Keys in 1827 when John Hodgson was the landlord. It was not until Peter Thornton took the public house over in 1885 that it became known as the Tramways Hotel. In 1888, it became known as the Tram Car Hotel, and when Andrew Nicol Dodds became the owner in 1894, it was then changed to the Tram Hotel, which stood on the corner of East Street. The Tram was badly damaged in October 1941, although there is a public house of that name in the market today. In the early years, when the town was a hamlet along the riverside, these streets were known as the Kings Highway. Thrift Street, formerly Commerce Street, was mainly the business sector of the town. Those streets were also known as the low end of the town.

From Harding's Bank, Spring Lane is to the right, Deer's Lane to the left. The Bee Hive public house, built in the 1700s, is the rounded building on the left. Originally called the Britannia Inn, Isaac Rodham was the landlord in 1827. The proprietor when the photograph was taken was Harry McDermott. In 1937, it had its licence refused and compensation of £1,837 was paid.

The Marquis of Lorne public house was on the corner of Thrift Street and Harding's Bank. Mary Ellen (Nelly) McFannan was the landlady. The small doorway to the left was an alley leading to the 'jug and bottle' department, where people took their own jug to be filled for taking home. In June 1906, the Justices refused to renew the licence and in April 1907 an appeal was dismissed. A further appeal to the King's Bench directed a re-hearing; upon that hearing on 15 June, a licence was granted by the Compensation Authority.

The Silent Woman public house was situated opposite Young's Dock, Wardle's Bank; its sign shows a decapitated female carrying her head under her arm. It was first advertised in 1839, when John Bell was landlord. In 1841, when advertised for sale, the Silent Woman had a cooper's shop and tenements adjoining. In 1853, William Thirkwe(a)ll advertises the public house as the Dock Inn. Ralph Grieves in 1854 called it the Dock, and when Thomas Wilson took over in 1856 he called it the Dock House Inn. When advertised for sale in 1857 it stated that it was formerly known as the Silent Woman.

On Thrift Street, opposite Dock Lane, was the Greenland Fishery public house. In 1827, Elizabeth Parker was the landlady; Charles Ranaut was the last landlord in 1872. According to Hodgson, on the opposite side of the road, facing the Greenland Fishery, was the Jolly Tar Inn.

One of the more unusual names for a public house, the Jolly Tar stood below Messrs Forsyth's Docks, at the head of Wardle's Bank. In 1867, Richard Thornton changed the name to the Harp Tavern and, when Joseph Chapman became the landlord in 1871, it became the Rector Inn; that was the last time it was advertised.

This is the south end of Thrift Street, looking east; the Union Flag Hotel is on the right. It was said that Jimmy Tracy, a well-known character in the Market Place prior to the First World War who was only 3 foot 4 inches tall, was so well known in the Union Flag that a chair had been specially heightened so he could reach the bar. In 1942, the licence was suspended and in April 1953 it was transferred to the Lake, Lake Avenue, Marsden.

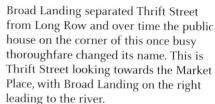

Broad Landing separated Thrift Street from Long Row and over time the public house on the corner of this once busy thoroughfare changed its name. This is Thrift Street looking towards the Market Place, with Broad Landing on the right leading to the river.

The Ship was in the hands of Cuthbert Bland from 1764 until he retired in 1779. Situated on the corner of Thrift Street and Broad Landing, it was possibly built in the early years of the town. In 1827, Alex Bains renamed the public house the Ship in Launch, a name it was to keep until 1877 when William Carlen Thompson, a master mariner was landlord. It possibly became the following establishment.

The Globe Hotel was first advertised in 1879 by Jeremiah Todhunter. The Globe lost its licence in August 1910, when compensation of £900 was paid. This later became the site of Brigham and Cowan's dock.

This lovely view of Long Rows cobbled street is looking to Burnt House Bank.

The Crown Inn goes back to 1726, according to the *Newcastle Courant*. Thomas Youens was landlord in the early 1800s, then Mary Ann Coats became landlady in 1827 and it was not advertised again.

The Burnt House was on the corner of Lower Thames Street and was originally called the Shipwright's Arms until 1841, when Ann Stobbs became the landlady and renamed it the Commercial Hotel. In 1873, Thomas Edmunds gave the address as Lower Thames Street. Its licence was transferred to the Eldon Arms in Eldon Street on 8 December 1932.

Wapping Street had a great number of 'Quays' running off the main street; Pan Ash Quay was the first, then Fairles' Quay, Half Moon Quay and Clayton's Quay, then Comical Corner. Next came Black Lion Quay, Hopper's Quay and Smith's Quay and then the Ferry Boat Landing, New Stairs and the Old Ferry Boat Landing, which was right next to Clarke's Quay and Middle Landing.

The Three Tuns Tavern was the only public house on Pan Ash, first advertised by Mrs Dunn in 1762, though it is possibly much older. Robert Dixon was the last to advertise the Three Tuns in 1866.

Fairles Quay had a number of public houses. The General Blucher Arms was owned by Ann Coulson in the early 1800s and the Ship Homer, which changed to the Ship, was owned by Margaret Liddell. The Albion was owned by Solomon Jewson in the 1830s. In 1839, the Trimmer's Arms appears, with John Laing as landlord. James Simm had the Stanhope & Tyne Tavern, which ceased in 1880, and in 1846 William Cook had the Fairles' Arms.

Wapping Street had many public houses. The Hope was owned by John Stephenson in 1794 and was changed to the Hope & Anchor by Benjamin Golightley in 1827, which he changed back to the Hope Tavern in 1828. There were also two Yorkshire Taverns next door to each other, the Melbourne Hotel, the Gray Horse, the Napoleon, the Phoenix Inn, the Dundee Arms, The Hermitage Inn, the Iron Ship Launch and the Blue Bell, to name but a few.

The Stirling Castle stood almost opposite the Newcastle House Inn. Francis Daniel, manager of the Stirling Castle from 1894, was also known for writing plays based on the hazardous occupations and the men who earned their living doing them on the riverside. Francis Daniel also wrote the book *The Angel of Comical Corner*. On 15 October 1936, the licence was transferred to the Sea Hotel, Sea Road.

The Newcastle House was built in the 1840s and rebuilt at the beginning of the 1870s. It belonged to William Sisterson from 1873 until his death. In 1919, his widow Eleanor mortgaged the pub to John Wilson. It stayed in the Wilson Family until it closed in 1930.

The Pine Apple Inn was another unusual name for a public house, Edward Jefferson being the landlord in 1860. On 4 March 1881, while owned by Robert Newland and occupied by Alexander Smithfield, the Pine Apple was burnt down and later rebuilt. On Tuesday 13 September 1887, John Carling woke to find the inn on fire; it was once again burnt to the ground and rebuilt for a second time. Unfortunately, on Friday 21 April 1893, while occupied by John Fraser, it was once again destroyed by fire and never rebuilt.

Sisterson's Burton House at Comical Corner had been called the Queen's Head when owned by Peter Henderson in 1827. In 1878, Robert Sisterson took over the Queen's Head Inn and by 1881 had renamed it Burton House. The Penny Ferry Landing can be seen to the right. Anna Mary Acheson was the last landlady in 1916.

According to the *Newcastle Courant* of 1791, Thomas Kirton gave the address of the Crown & Thistle (*centre*) as Kirton's Quay. In 1834, Mary Ann Reed gave the address as Wapping Street. In 1875, John Robert Bradley gave the address once again as Kirton's Quay; it later became Brigham & Cowan's Dry Docks.

Another quaint inn, named from a remarkable piece of sculpture above the door, the Noah's Ark Inn stood at the entrance to the old Ferry Landing opposite the foot of Long Bank. It is said that at that time (according to George B. Hodgson's *The History of South Shields*, 1903) it was the oldest public house in South Shields, having dated to at least Stewart times. It was better known as Bella Booth's, after Isabella Booth, who had been the landlady in the 1820s. In the 1830s it was as famous for its Ship Launch Dinners as it was for its ghosts. Its Long Room, curiously enough, held the first mission school in South Shields, as well as the meeting place for more than one religious body.

In 1827, Margaret Bell was the landlady of the Black Lion Inn, on Black Lion Quay. In 1856 Robert Branston Joseph called it the Lumpers Arms Inn but in 1862 William Cairn renamed it the Black Lion Inn once more. Brigham's Dock took over the site for shipbuilding.

Shadwell Street also had a number of Quays: Custom's House Quay, Cook's Quay, Salmon's Quay and Hospital Quay. There was also Coble Landing.

The Coble Inn was situated in an excellent position for the pilots and other seamen landing on the shore to refresh themselves before going home. In 1857, my husband's three-times-great grandmother, Elizabeth Phillips, was the landlady. Elizabeth kept the Coble until 1864, when James Croft became the landlord.

Shadwell Street had thirty-eight other public houses at one time. There were two Cobles, besides the one on Coble Landing, three Ships, two Black Bulls, a Hope and Anchor, a Boat, the Barley Mow, the Rose & Crown, the Three Tuns, a Duke of York, the Eclipse, the Rising Sun, a Newcastle Arms, Brown Anchor, Burlington Pier, the Globe, The Gray Horse, a Justice, The Lamb, the Star & Garter, Trinity Arms, the Half Moon, the Queen Victoria, Serenader's Arms, Hope & Anchor and the Elsinore Castle.

Pilot Street had a few public houses. The Rose and the Half Moon, having originally been in Pilot Street, then became part of Shadwell Street. The only public houses in Pilot Street were the Brown Cow, Creswell Hall, the Golden Fleece, the Yarmouth Arms, the Black Bull, the Coble, and yet another Ship.

There has been a public house on the Lawe since Cross House or Lawe House was erected. Apparently, at the beginning of the nineteenth century, the Baltic Tavern stood on the site of an even older tavern.

As far back as 1726, there has been a Crown Inn in the town, although whether it was the one on the Lawe here or the one in Long Row it is not clear.

The Crown Inn consisted of a front parlour, a sitting room, (which overlooks one of the best views in the town), a tap room, a bar and a cellarage on the ground floor, with bedrooms above.

The first time the Crown Inn was advertised was in 1834 by Mary Reed (and she gave the address as 1 Lawe Buildings). Mary Hart took over the Crown in 1839, giving the address as 'The Sea Side'. The Crown Inn was not advertised again until 1853, when Mrs Mary Chambers gave the address as Beacon Street. It has been said that at one time it was occupied by James Cook, whose family were the landlords that sold it in the latter half of the 1800s, but I have found no evidence of this. James Cook died in 1779 and James Henry Cook was not the landlord until 1881. Today it is known as the Harbour Lights and has recently been refurbished.

The Beacon Inn, first advertised in 1853 by Anthony Percy, stands on the site of an old rope works. The Beacon, which takes its name from the 1832 beacon that ships used as a marker, commands an exceptional view, which over the last 100 years has changed a great deal, with all the old streets below having been pulled down in the last century; even the property next to it has gone.

The Look Out Inn is on what was originally called St Stephens Street, now Fort Street. The Look Out goes back to between the late 1700s to the early 1800s and was first advertised in 1821, when the landlord was James Baity. In 1857 John Weatherburn renamed the inn as the Pilot's Look Out Inn, possibly because of the clear view from the upper room windows of the mouth of the Tyne. The pilots would sit at the window in the warmth, thanks to the hospitality of the landlord, and still be able to see any distress signals from ships at sea. Over the years, like many other public houses, it has had to keep up to date with the trends of its clientele. The door to the right was the jug and bottle.

Inside the Look Out, Tony Strong, a patron, told me that in the 1950s there was a centre bar that served the three rooms; the bar is now where the corridor to the pilots' room at the back used to be.

The Turk's Head had been in Military Road since 1843, when Margaret Hilton was the landlady, and it was owned by Sarah Green. Situated high up at the top of the Pilot Stairs, it looked over brisk activities on the streets and river below.

In 1809, Mrs Smith gave the address of the Bee Hive Inn as 'Bank Top', when on Tuesday 12 December a 'Public or Vestry Meeting was held there'. It was said that it had a picture of a bee hive with the motto,

> In this bee hive we're all alive,
> Good liquor makes us funny.
> If you are dry, come and try
> The flavour of our honey.

In 1897, plans were passed to rebuild the Bee Hive Inn. The address was then Wellington Street.

The *Gazette* on 4 February 1952 stated:

> As the Ministry of Housing and Local Government has refused as application by the brewery company for a licence for a new public house in the place of the company's Bee Hive Inn which is on the site of proposed flats at Wellington Street, and the Ministry has suggested that the Town Council should proceed with the erection of the three of the four blocks of flats, part of the garden at the rear of the Bee Hive Inn will be acquired, it had been reported to the Housing Committee.

The Bee Hive Inn we know today is in Mile End Road and is a more modern public house, looking out across St Stephen's church and grave yard to the Tyne beyond.

Above: Although Mile End Road ran from Long Bank to the junction of Ocean Road and King Street, it only ever had two public houses.

Originally called the Mile End Tavern, this pub was opened at the end of the 1830s by Henry Newbigin, built on the corner of Bath Street and Mile End Road. It was not until 1869 that it became the Mile End Station Hotel, while under the management of Joseph Gowland. After the Second World War, it became known simply as the Station Hotel.

Right: Built much later than the Station Hotel, the North Eastern Hotel was opened by Ralph Henderson in 1872. In 1987, landlord Brian Smith opened what was thought to be the first separate games room for the public. Although the building is still there, it ceased trading as a public house many years ago and lately it was a coffee house.

In 1856, the Garrick's Head, standing on the corner of Queen Street and Salem Street, was up for sale; it was described as an old, established inn and spirit vaults. George Jones was the first to advertise the Garrick's Head in 1865. Thomas Edgar Middleton was the last landlord recorded in the licensing book. The Garrick's Head stood on the site of what is now the car park of the NatWest bank.

The Black and Grey, built at the beginning of the 1800s, was on the corner of North Street and Union Alley. The name was said to derive from the colour of the horses that once pulled the mail coaches to and from the coaching hotels, the Rose and Crown in the Market Place and the Golden Lion in King Street. First advertised by John Wilkinson in 1827, this beautiful building was rebuilt in 1900 under the ownership of Rowell & Sons Ltd. with the address as No. 41 Union Alley. It graced the entrance of this once vibrant thoroughfare until it was demolished in 1973. An Italian restaurant, Bravi, now stands on the site.

Union Alley was once a busy thoroughfare with many businesses and a theatre.

Starting as the Travellers' Arms, this pub opened at the beginning of the 1800s and in 1827 John Tutton was the landlord. By 1828, John had changed the name to the Blue Anchor. By 1834, John had changed it back to the Travellers' Arms. In 1841, Ann Weatherall had taken over the public house and renamed it Shades. By 1848, Isaiah Brimer had changed the name to the Sawyer's Arms Inn, but in 1850, Mrs Ann Brown called the public house the Queen's Head Inn. In 1897, Rowell & Sons Ltd. applied for planning permission to rebuild the Queen's Head, which was granted in July that year.

In 1900, John Kemp Hall changed the name of the Queen's Head and it became the Imperial Hotel. This advert is from the South Shields Year Book 1902. Like the Market Place, Union Alley was hit by enemy bombs in October 1941 and was badly damaged. On 5 December 1957, the licence was transferred to the Grey Hen on the corner of Harton Lane.

The Empire Vaults, built by Richard Thornton in the 1870s as the Shakespeare

The Imperial Hotel

(FREE HOUSE).

UNION ALLEY, SOUTH SHIELDS.

The most Up-to-Date House IN THE NORTH OF ENGLAND.

BAR.   BUFFET.   BILLIARDS.

A 4-Course Dinner supplied Daily between 12 & 3.
ONE SHILLING.
N.B.—The above is served up in capital style and is a challenge to the world.

McEWAN'S AND RITCHIE'S 90s SPECIAL ALES.
BASS ON DRAUGHT.
Wines, Spirits and Cigars are of the same excellent quality.

The whole Business is under the personal superintendence of the

PROPRIETOR,

JOHN K. HALL

(ONE OF YOURSELVES).

Nat. Tel. No. 19.

Inn, was once part of the Empire Theatre. By 1880, Richard Thornton had renamed the inn Burton Cellars No. 2, but in 1881 he called it the Shakespeare Inn once again. In 1900, Alexander Bell renamed the public house the Empire Vaults. In 1912, the owners did not apply for the renewal of the licence and it was closed.

King Street was originally built at the end of the 1700s and only went as far as Waterloo Vale. The numbers went up on the north side and then down on the south side. In 1827, King Street had six public houses.

The Scarbro' Spa was built next to the Old Highlander in the late 1790s at the Market Place end of King Street. In 1855, Stephen Falp, my three-times-great grandfather, was the landlord; he stayed for four years. Alexander Deucher bought the public house in 1890 and in 1900 it was also known as a music saloon. In 1938, he submitted plans to rebuild the Scarbro' Spa and these were passed in 1940. The Scarbro' Spa closed in 1958 and the licence was transferred to the Jester, Tasmania Road.

In 1827, Richard Walton had the 'Highlander' in King Street and by 1834 he had called it the Old Highlander. In 1865, Walter Curle gave the address as Union Alley, where the public house also had an entrance. In 1877, William Jackson, the owner, was granted planning permission to alter the pub and it was rebuilt in 1878. The Highlander closed in the 1960s and was converted into a shop; it is the building we know today as Vision Express.

Built by Richard Rain in 1794 as the New Inn, it was described in the *Newcastle Courant* on 18 October 1794 as 'a large, elegant and commodious house, with every necessary convenience situated at the east end of King Street. Leading from the said Market Place, to Sunderland Road; having fitted out the same in a proper manner, and laid in a large assortment of Wines, Spirituous and other Liquors, of the best quality and hopes, by his assiduity and good accommodations to his Friends to merit their approbation. N. B. Good Stabling within the Premises.'

Edward Cleugh bought the hotel in May 1798 but he did not stay long. On Monday 25 November 1799, all the household goods and effects of the inn were sold and on the Wednesday the carriages and hay were also sold. Taken over by John Oyston in January 1800, the Golden Lion had once again taken a prestigious place in the community. In 1803, the first stage coach ran from the Golden Lion to York. The Golden Lion stayed in the Oyston family for more than fifty years and, although Thomas Oyston Jnr took no part in the day-to-day running of the hotel, the family retained it.

John Gray Weir had The Golden Lion rebuilt in 1875 on the site formerly occupied by the old established hotel. The old premises, which were still to the rear of the new hotel, were then pulled down to build new premises

GOLDEN LION HOTEL

(Proprietors: Alexander Deuchar Ltd.   Phone 79.

First - Class Family & Commercial Hotel

King Street   -   SOUTH SHIELDS.

Commanding position, close to Railway Station, Ferry and Post Office.   Handsome Grill Room.   Table d'Hote Luncheon 12 to 3 p.m.   Magnificent Banqueting Hall and Ball Room.   Orchestral Balcony.   Dining accommodation for over 200 guests.   Special Dinners.   Banquets. Wedding Breakfasts a Speciality.   Day and Night Porters. Excellent Cuisine.   Fine Selection of Wines.

comprising a large bar and restaurant, with billiard room and assembly room above. The new stable and coach house made this one of the largest buildings in the town. Alexander Deuchar was probably the last of the entrepreneurs to own the Golden Lion and he made it into the hotel many will remember, operating over the next fifty years as Alex Deuchar Ltd. Taken over by Scottish & Newcastle Breweries, the Golden Lion and the King Hall Assembly Room in North Street thrived for many more years, and in 1963 it was modernised and improved, with the intention that it would last for many more. Unfortunately, in 1971, Parkers (Caterers) North East Ltd. did not get their lease renewed; they had opened the King's Hall Assembly Rooms in 1954. The closure of the Golden Lion saw the demise of nearly 200 years of local history, from the French Revolution through the early years of the Royal Mail stagecoaches. It could also tell of the many inquests, auctions and bankruptcys that had been heard within its walls. Once a typical Dickensian inn, the Oyston family made it the centre of social life in the town, which it never lost over the next 150 years.

Built in the early 1800s, this pub was originally called the Masons' Arms and first advertised in 1827 by John Hart. In 1875, Thomas Sharp advertised No. 72 King Street as the Eagle Inn. In 1894, William Jackson called the public house the Eagle Vaults.

The Eagle Vaults had a long bar running from King Street to East Street; businessmen of the town wearing frock coats and top hats would use the main entrance in King Street, while the East Street entrance was used by the cloth-capped working men. The long bar (35 yards) had a period piece of mahogany and glass panelling, an invisible line between the two classes of customer. The Bodega was an annex of the Eagle, a kind of raised wine cellar, opened for an exclusive clientele of businessmen and professional people who enjoyed sampling superior wines. It had to close at 6 p.m., a condition made by magistrates. Its wines were drawn from the wood and the wine tasters came in great numbers from all around, bringing their tall silk hats with them. Tables and chairs of any kind were taboo; there were upturned casks or an empty box, but that was all. The Eagle was closed in 1968.

The Forrester's Arms was not as old as the Masons' Arms, dating from the 1840s, when Sarah Jobling first advertised the public house in 1846. By 1868, the Forrester's Arms was no longer in King Street and the back had been renamed the Mechanics' Hotel.

The Lord Collingwood **was** built when King Street was first formed in about 1795/6; see the Lambton Arms, East Street.

Built later than King Street, East King Street had four original public houses: the King's Head, Mariners Arms, the Neptune and the Turf Inn.

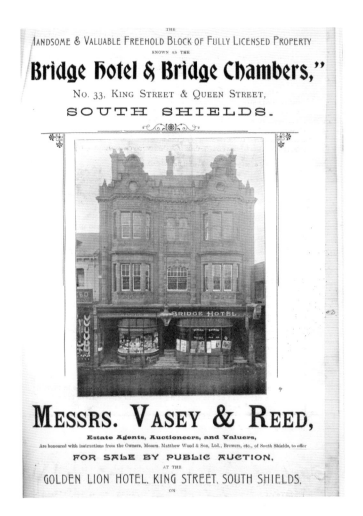

THE

HANDSOME & VALUABLE FREEHOLD BLOCK OF FULLY LICENSED PROPERTY

KNOWN AS THE

Bridge Hotel & Bridge Chambers,"

No. 33, KING STREET & QUEEN STREET,

SOUTH SHIELDS.

MESSRS. VASEY & REED,

Estate Agents, Auctioneers, and Valuers,

Are honoured with instructions from the Owners, Messrs. Matthew Wood & Son, Ltd., Brewers, etc., of South Shields, to offer

FOR SALE BY PUBLIC AUCTION,

AT THE

GOLDEN LION HOTEL. KING STREET. SOUTH SHIELDS.

ON

Originally the King's Head when it was built, William Hartland first advertised this property in 1821. In 1839, Isabella Story became landlady and the public house became known as the Bridge Inn. The name was possibly due to the building of the first bridge over East King Street to convey the Stanhope and Tyne railway line from Stanhope to the river, linking the Weardale and north-west Durham coal & lime reserves with the Tyne. The inn was quite an antiquated old place that passengers had to pass through on their way to board the train; before boarding the train they would purchase their ticket in the back room of the inn, before the railway station in Mile End Road was built.

The Bridge closed around 1973, but if you walk along Queen Street you can still make out the lettering on the tiles, or look up under the bridge in King Street and see the gargoyles on either side of the building.

On the corner of Waterloo Vale stood the Coach and Horses Inn, which was not only the first public house built in East King Street, but also the first building. It was originally called the Brick and Tile Inn from its proximity to Mr Nicholas Fairles's tile sheds, which at that time stood behind it. Joseph Sinnott, who was the landlord, lost his licence for allowing drunken fights to take place between the Irish workers working for Mr Fairles. John Pickering took over the public house in 1844 and renamed it the Coach and Horses Inn in 1846. The Coach and Horses Inn was the old posting house of the town; the landlord John Pickering was also a cab proprietor. The pub became Wigham's drapers; today it is Dunn's, the tailors.

It was not until 1887 that George Milburn, as proprietor, advertised the Scotia at No. 42 ½ King Street. It was possibly named after a vessel owned by Cllr Joseph Lawson, which set sail from the Tyne for Scarborough in 1884. This beautiful photograph shows both the old Scotia, which was pulled down for the widening of Mile End Road, and the one we know today. Planning permission was granted on 7 January 1903 for the rebuilding of the Scotia, which resulted in the building we see today.

This was one of many public houses and a hotel owned by Alexander Deuchar Ltd. but is the only one surviving in King Street from a long forgotten past.

In 1873, George Deuchar first advertised the Tiger Inn as the Board Hotel; by the next year, Mrs Ann Elizabeth Deuchar, wine and spirit merchant, was the owner. In 1887, John William Barlow took over the Board. In 1894, Robert Emmerson renamed the hotel the Tiger Inn, which is the building next to what is now McDonalds. In 1899, J. Chipchase & Co. owned the Tiger and in 1900 Walter Palethorpe advertised the inn as the Victoria Inn. In 1908, it was taken over by the North Eastern Banking Co. and was later pulled down for the widening of Fowler Street.

Originally called German Street, there were only two very old public houses, the Spring Garden Tavern and the German Cottage Inn. Other hotels and taverns were built later.

Originally called the Albion, which was given the address of No. 2 Fowler Street, William Matthews first advertised the public house in 1839. Rebuilt and designed to replicate the Criterion Grill in London, it was originally a restaurant and refreshment room, to cater for the ladies and gentlemen of the town. Jeremiah Todhunter, proprietor in 1877, catered for both businessmen and families, who would dine on dishes of chops and roast dinners. In 1888, when William Jackson became proprietor, the Criterion had also become a grill room with an extensive menu.

When entering the Criterion just after it closed in 2012, the upper floor looked as if time had stood still; you could imagine the room being full of well-dressed patrons gathering for lunch or dinner in this once frequented room. The clocks William Jackson had installed in 1885 were still on the walls, although one had stopped at 11.38 and the other at 3.30, and glasses were still on the bar waiting to be washed by the bar staff when they arrived for their next shift.

Better known as the Ship & Royal than as the Royal Hotel, this once beautiful hotel was first advertised by Mark Rest in the 1879 directory. In 1885, Farquhar M. Laing reopened the Royal as the Royal Grill after the hotel had stood empty for most of the early part of 1880s, and restored it to its former glory. In 1903, the Royal Hotel was altered and changes were made to upgrade it by the adding of sanitary conveniences to the back. From the 1930s and '40s, my grandmother's sister Margaret (Maggie) Curry and then my husband's aunt, Violet (Vi) Burnett, worked there as housekeepers and then as the hotel manageresses. Over the years, the Royal has undergone many changes and many owners. Some will remember it as 'MARR'S corner', while some may remember it as a hotel but not as the once beautiful building it once was. In January 1969, the Royal as a hotel was put up for sale by public auction and the contents sold. No longer a hotel, the ground floor is better known as the Ship & Royal and the upper floors are a nightclub.

The Grapes Hotel was built at the end of the 1860s and according to the 1871 directory John Parker was the first landlord, calling the hotel the New Grapes Hotel, as he had been landlord of the Grapes Hotel in the Market Place. This beautiful Victorian building, once described as a great rambling place, stood on the corner of Ocean Road and Woodbine Street. In 1883, planning permission was granted for an extension to the hotel, which was owned by William Jackson at the time and managed by James Bamber. Over the years, the hotel underwent many changes and many landlords. At some stage, it had part of the floor removed into the cellar to make a dining area. At one time, the hotel became known as the Balancing Eel and over the years has had several changes of name, being called Stage Set and Benders before being given the latest name of the Bizz Bar. Closed for many years, this once beautiful hotel stood derelict on the corner of a once thriving thoroughfare of shops and businesses, which now are mostly Indian restaurants.

Sadly, around 5.30 p.m. on Friday 9 March 2012 this once proud Victorian hotel became another relic of a bygone era and collapsed.

Built at the end of the 1840s, William Metcalf first advertised the German Cottage in 1850 as a beer house, which stood opposite Roman Road. In 1875, Thomas Stebbings, a master mariner, then became the landlord. It is supposed to have been the scene of several murders and reputed to have been the haunt of smugglers, but by 1880 it had been pulled down and a church built on the site.

Planning permission was granted on 15 April 1875 for the building of a new hotel at the side of the German Cottage Tavern. The Pier Hotel was first advertised by James Wilkinson in 1879, when the address was given as No. 12 Glover Terrace. James Wilkinson kept the Pier until 1889, when John Tulley took it over, but he did not stay long as in 1891 Robert Lockey was then the landlord. In 1894, William Harle became the landlord and when he left in 1913 the address became No. 154 Ocean Road. The landlord, Stephen FizMaurice, has been at the Pier for sixteen years. The Pier, like many of the older public houses, has a traditional long bar that was originally on the left of the door; at the far end of the bar was an opening which served as the 'jug and bottle', and in later years the women that did not want to come in would stand there and drink their schooner of ale.

The front was the snug, and the back was the public bar; the original glass panel can still be seen. Below is the original hatch from the end of the bar.

Built around 1870, the Marine Hotel was first advertised in 1871 by George Thompson, the address being No. 20 Pier Terrace. In 1873, the Marine was advertised as being 'situated in the most healthy part of South Shields, commanding a fine view of the mouth of the Tyne, and an extensive view of the German Ocean. It is adjoining the New Promenade Pier, and the extensive sea-bathing Beach, where every accommodation for bathers is provided, and only a short distance from Marsden Rock.' Today, it stands beside the Marine Parks and the new leisure pool.

Built in the early 1850s, James Burt was the landlord of the Woodbine Hotel in 1856; he gave the address as East Catherine Street, which was on the corner of Woodbine Street. In 1905, planning permission was passed for a urinal and WC to be built in the yard of the Woodbine Hotel. Like the rest of the area, the Woodbine was pulled down for to make way for the new Woodbine estate.

The Lord Nelson stood on the corner of Alma Street and Woodbine Street, adjacent to the Woodbine Hotel. The Lord Nelson was a popular pub and, in its latter years, was apparently well known for its feathered resident, a parrot named Bobby, who was given to encouraging customers with a cheerful 'have a beer' and who would also give a passable rendition of 'Shake, Rattle and Roll'! The last entry in the licence book was on 4 December 1974.

Built on the corner of Catherine Street in the late 1840s as the Rope Maker's Arms, Mary Ann Purvis first advertised this pub in 1848. Standing across the street to the Lord Nelson, it was not until 1900 that it was first advertised as the Catherine House by James George Mole. Better known as the 'Monkey Bar' in its latter years, the last entry was on 2 February 1961.

Built around the middle of the 1850s, Richard Dockwray first advertised the Stag's Head Inn in 1857; the address was given as No. 10. As Fowler Street became more popular and more property was built, the street numbers, instead of going up on one side and down the other, started being numbered as we know today and the Stags Head became No. 51 in 1861.

Rebuilt in 1897, the Stag's Head has two bars, one long room downstairs that was extended to the outside perimeter in the 1970s and a smaller, cosy bar upstairs. It is the only one of the four public houses that were situated in Fowler Street in the late 1800s to exist today. Changing to keep up with the demands of the twenty-first century, it has managed to retain that old world look, with its original long bar that was installed when it was rebuilt over 110 years ago. Michael FizMaurice, the manager, is always on hand to make his clientele welcome.

The Wheat Sheaf Hotel was built on the corner of Fowler Street and Smithy Street as early as 1837; Elizabeth Jameson was the first landlady to advertise the public house in 1839. On 16 July 1903, the amended plans were passed for the rebuilding of the Wheat Sheaf; this was due to the plans for the widening of Fowler Street, which saw the buildings on the west side of the street demolished. This beautiful architectural building had mullioned windows, balustrade balconies and a fantastic beautiful turret on top. Unfortunately, the building was demolished for the widening of Keppel Street.

The Royal Arms in Albemarle Street was at one time owned by Alex Deuchar Ltd. First advertised in 1873, it had a white tiled façade and, in later years, became known as the Albemarle after the name of the street. In the early years, it did not seem to keep its landlords for very long. From 1873 to 1900, it had nine landlords, the longest staying for around six years. Annie McCarthy's now stands on the site and was formerly known as the Albemarle, the name most people had used for the Royal Arms.

In 1827, George Turner was the owner of the Free Gardeners Arms on Westoe Lane. In 1834, it was renamed the Gardeners Arms.

On 19 May 1859, planning permission was approved for Robert Bell to build a new public house on the site near what was called the Jingling Gate. This was opposite Albion Terrace, near the corner of Claypath Lane and Westoe Lane, where the junction was marked with a gatepost made from the jawbone of a whale; it was said that if closed in a hurry it would swing with a peculiar knocking sound, which gave it the name. It was at that time surrounded by fields, with nothing to the south until Westoe Village and nothing to the east but the Golden Babby farmhouse, at the corner of what was Winchester Street. The hotel commanded a splendid view.

Rebuilt in 1898 into this beautiful building, it included bathrooms, which at the time was classed as very modern. Mrs Elizabeth Hamilton Mitchell was the first landlady to advertise it in 1898. The Britannia took its name from the royal seal of approval of the late nineteenth century and has retained its famous regal name to this day, in spite of many other changes in the area around the pub. By the mid-1930s, the Britannia was bought by John Rowell & Son Limited, a wine and spirit merchant, and many changes were being made in the area; the old properties were being replaced with better housing.

A statue of Britannia used to stand where the board now is. Britannia originally stood in the lounge of the liner *Mauretania* and lost both hands and head through vandalism. Today, the Britannia still stands proud on this now busy thoroughfare.

Originally called the George Inn, this inn was built on the corner of West Keppel Street and Waterloo Vale and owned by George Heslop in 1846. It was not until Ralph Buglass took over the George in 1859 that he renamed the pub the Havelock Inn. In 1884, Mrs Mary Buglass changed the name to the General Havelock. In February 1957, Annie Mason Lynch became the landlady and stayed until it was pulled down and moved for the widening of Keppel Street. The new public house was again named the Havelock and it was pulled down in 2012. Below is a glimpse inside the old General Havelock when Annie Mason Lynch was the landlady in the 1960s.

In 1857, the only public house in Barrington Street was the Salmon Inn at No. 21. In 1879, Edward Wood had taken over the Salmon Inn and it was in 1883 that it became the Spirit Vaults at No. 10 Barrington Street. In 1887, Richard Jeffels renamed the public house the Buffalo Hotel; this name is thought to be from either the Wild West Show of Buffalo Bill Cody or from the RAOB (Royal Antediluvian Order of the Buffalo), originally called the Buffaloes. Capt William Davison became the owner in 1894 and in 1897 it became the Douglas Inn, later becoming the Douglas Vaults and better known as the Dougie. When sold by auction on 11 October 1899 it had the following description:

> Having a frontage of 23 feet 6 inches and a depth of 51 feet or thereabouts, and containing very large Bar, Smoke Room, Two Snuggs, lange Yard and every modern converience, all on the Ground Floor. In the Basement is a large and lofty Cellar, and on the First Floor very large Smoke Room or Billiard Roon, and the Second Floor, Three good Tooms and Scullery.

In 2013, the Douglas Vaults was completely refurbished, both internally and externally, and has now become the Cross Arms Hotel. Part of the new image are the new Real Ales that it has started to keep, these being mainly national brands. It also advertises accommodation, live music on Friday and Saturday nights, sports television and a smoking area.

East Street was at one time a very narrow street, not much wider than a dray wagon, and was known as the 'kill or cure street' because of the number of doctors' surgeries.

Originally called the Star Inn, this public house dates back to the mid-1800s and was first advertised by Thomas Barrass in 1865. It was not until after the Star Inn was rebuilt in 1899, with 'shops and arcade in King Street and Dining Room above', that Christian Marsh changed the name to the Avenue Hotel. This photograph is of the King Street entrance. In the late 1940s, the Avenue Bar was in East Street and customers would gain access through a beautiful arcade that was situated in King Street.

The Avenue had a beautifully decorated interior and the upstairs lounge had a huge glass dome, which formed part of the ceiling in the early days.

This beautiful glittering interior of ornate tiles and a frieze depicting a garland of fruit was uncovered when Hepworth, the tailors, were having a revamp of the store. It is said that art students would often go into the bar to sketch it.

One of only two public houses left in what was once a thriving thoroughfare, the Mechanics' Arms in East Street has changed little over the last few years. Going in, on the left is what would have been the snug and the right is the bar area. Gina, the landlady, is very friendly and her husband, John, has the Lambton Arms next door.

Above is shown the snug bar on the left-hand side of the Mechanics' Arms.

Originally called the Lord Collingwood and built around 1795/6, it was in the hands of John Dunn until it was taken over by Archibald Mitchelson in 1835 and he changed it to Lambton Arms. Archibald Mitchelson was also a brewer, brewing his own ale and porter for selling to his clientele. In 1875, Marshall Grey advertised the public house as the Phoenix but the next year he renamed it the City of Glasgow. Since being rebuilt in 1892, the public house has changed little over the centuries and still maintains an old world look about it. Once known as Smugglers, it again changed its name back to the Lambton Arms. Inside the Lambton Arms there is a small bar at the back and it has retained many of its original features. It carries one of the largest displays of whisky I have seen in one place outside of Scotland. Listed by CAMRA, three beers, including Bass, are available and this popular public house is busy at times. Opening at 7 a.m., it has a warm, friendly atmosphere and always welcomes its clientele.

The whiskey bottles can be seen on the wall on the right-hand side of the bar.

Originally called the Engine House, the address was Mill Dam and in 1834 William Dand changed the name to the Crown Glass Works Inn, probably because of the glass works across the road. By 1855, William Copeland, a cart proprietor, had renamed the tavern the Crown Glass Tavern. It was rebuilt in 1859 by John Barrass, and in 1861, William Ingoe changed the name to the Glass House Tavern. W. Scouler & Co. advertised the public house in 1875 as the Customs House Tavern, as seen here in 1939 with the chimney of the glass works in the background.

The Trimmers Arms, built on the corner of Hill Street, was first advertised in 1879 by James Gray. Although rebuilt in 1891, the Trimmers lost its licence and compensation was paid on 24 August 1910, when it became a shop. In 2004, opening once more, it was refurbished as a restaurant and public house. It incorporated the old Trimmers Arms premises and those of the West End Vaults next door.

West End Vaults were opened in 1870 by Metcalfe & Sons and in 1890 alterations were carried out on the public house. At one time it was also known as the Tyne Lodge. Unfortunately, the public house was badly burnt in the 1990s.

The Waggon Inn was first mentioned in 1827 by landlord Robert Cook. In 1844, Revd R. H. Holmes of the Holy Trinity church wrote, 'The father of Mr J. C. Stephenson began a school in the now disused station for the sons of men employed at his Chemical Factory. One for the girls was held in the Waggon Inn. This school developed in to the well-known Barnes School.' William Gibson was landlord of the Waggon Inn from 1839 to 1862. The Waggon Inn closed in 1928 after the owner R. Spence of Westoe Parade died and the licence expired on 25 August.

Portberry Street was opposite Weetman Street, where the Commercial Tavern once stood and the Wagon Way Inn was situated. Thomas Henderson advertised the Wagon Way Inn for the first time in 1865, possibly taking its name from the Wagon Way, which ran across the top of the street, and then under Commercial Road to the Glass Works by the river. In 1894, my great-great grandmother, Mary Jane Ferguson, was the landlady of the Wagon Inn after leaving the Old Station Hotel in Laygate Lane.

The Neptune Hotel was built at the junction of Corstorphine Town, Commercial Road, facing north to the shipyards on the Tyne at the start of West Holborn. It would seem that this hotel was built opposite the Neptune Inn that was in Corstorphine Town. The hotel was possibly built to replace the inn, which became a good watering hole for the shipyard workers. In 1987, the bailiffs were called in when the manager at the time left, leaving money owing to the brewery; this was the beginning of the end for the pub.

Originally called the Earl Gray, this public house was first advertised in 1841 by Esther Lumley. It kept the Earl Gray name until its licence was surrendered on 2 February 1961. Reopening as the Dolly Peel, named after a legendary fishwife and smuggler, it has changed with the times and serves a more mature clientele than that when it first opened. The original bar has unfortunately been removed, but the new one is still in keeping with the atmosphere of the old; divided into two areas, the bar, as you enter by the front of the Dolly Peel, is a small but cosy room with a large television for sporting events.

The snug is a welcoming room off the main bar with a bookcase and numerous books, which I am sure you would be welcome to read; it can be entered from the car park to the side of the pub.

Originally built as the Laygate Inn, it was first advertised by Luke Todd in 1848. In 1865, Isaac Coulson became the landlord and in 1875 changed the name to the Station Hotel; this photograph by the Harton Coal Company was taken in October 1891. The photograph in the window is Thomas Ferguson, who had been licensee until his death in August that year. His wife, Mary Jane, my great-great-grandmother, took over the running of the hotel. The M. J. has been newly painted over the 'T'.

Above is Station Hotel as it is today. The doors and windows of the pub have been replaced by a double door and much smaller windows. The premises are now the workshop of John Nichol fabrications. The rest of the streets that were once behind it have long gone, as well as the train lines that once carried the coal to Harton Staiths. Although the building has been split into three units, a broken cask still lies in the cellar of what is now a car repair centre.

The High Station Hotel, on the corner of Eldon Street, was built as a replacement for the Station Hotel above but, like so many of the hotels in the area, it closed due to the decline of the houses and people being moved to the new estates to the south of the town. The new Station Hotel was closed in June 1959; its licence was transferred to the Bamburgh Arms, Bamburgh Avenue.

The Eldon Arms was built on the corner of Barnes Road and Eldon Street, opposite Barnes Road School. This impressive building was first advertised in 1900 by James Robson. The Eldon Arms lost its licence and compensation was paid to the owners on 3 August 1929, when plans were submitted to convert this once splendid building into dwellings.

The old Garden Gate was probably built on the site of the gardens of Lay House, known as No.1 Broken Gardens, from which the name is thought to derive. The one here was rebuilt as a hotel on the corner of Taylor Street; it was in many ways a pub of great antiquity. A popular pastime for its clientele besides drinking was playing quoits, and it was famous for its cycling fraternity. Behind the Garden Gate there was also a brewery, once kept by James Watt, which it is said had a line straight into the cellar and produced the only ale sold.

According to G. B. Hodgson, the South Shields historian, the gravestone of Ralph Milborne, draper, who died in 1668, was discovered in the garden of the public house during alterations. The Adam and Eve once stood among green fields in what was a very sparsely populated part of the town. Thought to have been built in the grounds of the seventeenth-century private house belonging to Ralph Milburn, the land had a long association with Quaker burials. The Adam & Eve is known to have been a tavern in the hands of John Rowell in the early 1820s.

The rate of £8 a quarter was paid on the property, which was quite a large sum in 1850. Margaret Raffle was the landlady at that time. Although owned by John Clay, first mayor of South Shields, John I'Anson, an ale and porter merchant, became the licensee in 1856. At one point, John Clay offered to sell the tavern to John I'Anson for £250, which he supposedly declined. In 1857, John I'Anson is given as the owner, when planning permission was granted to extend the outbuildings and the tombstone came to light. This old photograph was taken when John I'Anson held the licence. The Adam & Eve has been serving the community for almost 200 years and is still open today.

The Duke of York public house is to the left on the corner of Green Street and George Street. Opened around 1850 by Isaac Henzell, the Duke of York was 'beer only' and 'popular with those who preferred their refreshments in a smaller type of Inn'; it stood on the corner of a busy thoroughfare that stayed unchanged until 1940, when it closed its doors for the last time.

Judging by the 1856 map of South Shields, the Bath Hotel was built on the site of the old Bath and Washhouses in what was John Street. Originally built in the late 1850s, the landlord was John Munroe. The 'Bath' closed in 1954.

Looking towards the corner of Smith Street, the Mosque, which was once the Hilda Tavern, was opened in 1865 by George Bamborough. The tavern was rebuilt in 1898 as the Hilda Arms, as the plaque on the wall tells us: 'Hilda Arms Rebuilt 1898.' After being rebuilt, the Hilda Arms was only open another thirty years before surrendering its licence on 21 March 1928. The Arab community converted the bar into their prayer room and they bathed in the converted beer cellar. The sign on the Mosque then read 'Mosque for all Muslims' in both Arabic and English.

Opened around 1865 by John Briscoe, the Lord Clyde has stood virtually unchanged over the last 155 years. The Lord Clyde was granted a billiard licence in September 1887 and was the first to do so. The Lord Clyde was well known for its concert room, but in 1986 it was taken over and given a complete facelift, both the bar and lounge now being 'L' shaped rooms. It is now the Bar Blue.

In 1839, Edward Anderson owned a board, 'a licence premise with no name', which stood on the corner of Claypath Lane. In 1848, William Anderson took over as licensee, and by 1850 he had named his board the Queen's Head Hotel. It was rebuilt in 1906 by W. B. Reid & Co. into the very impressive building you can see in the centre of this photograph. When the Queen's Head closed in 1954, the licence was transferred to the Mariner, Mortimer Road, but it remained standing for quite a few years.

Standing at Laygate end of Adelaide Street, the Benton Inn first comes to light in 1865 when George Foreman was the landlord. The Benton Inn stood in what was a thriving street in the Laygate area of the town; it was also one of the smaller public houses in the area.

The Old Mill Inn was not always an inn but started life as a working mill, dating back to 1744. Owned by Ship owner Robert Green in the 1800s, his widow sold the land to Thomas Reay in 1848. The land in the area was for housing but the Mill, which was supposed to come down, survived and was bought by Richard and Peter Thornton to manufacture mineral water. It was not until 1900, when George Hornby held the licence, that the Old Mill Inn appeared in a directory. When the licence was suspended in 1956 it was transferred to the New Mill, Biddick Hall.

The Queen's Head stood on the corner of Raglan Street and Princes Street, part of the newly built area of Laygate. Opened in 1870 by James Wilson, it stayed in the family for fifteen years until it was taken over by the Turnbull family, who again kept the licence for the next ten years. The Queen's Head was rebuilt in 1904 by Rowell & Sons, who were the owners at that time with Henry Fail as the landlord. The licence was suspended on 29 March 1957.

Looking down Bedford Street from Laygate Lane, the Prince Albert is in the centre, with the Mill Inn to the right. The Prince Albert, built on the corner of Orange Street, was opened in 1873 by William Havelock; on 26 April 1957, the licence was suspended and it closed for the last time.

The Volunteer Arms in Cambridge Street was owned by John Turnbull, brewers; although not much to look at it was a very popular drinking hole for people far and wide. The Volunteer looked more like a converted house than a purpose-built inn. Opened in the 1890s, Thomas Wase was the landlord. The pub first became known as Pinkney's before the Second World War, when George Waterton Pickney was the owner in 1924 and landlord from 1929 to 1940. During the war it was used to billet the officers of the Royal Air Force while in charge of a Barrage Balloon site. After the war it was better known as 'Abadan's'; I have been told that the landlord had once sailed the seven seas, mostly to the Persian Gulf on tankers. This may have been George Diggle, who became the landlord in 1946.

Planning permission for The Chichester Arms was granted at the end of August 1876. The address in 1880 was No. 1 Chichester Road and No. 5 Alexander Terrace; Ralph Hodge Thompson was the licensee. Chichester has seen many changes over the 135 years since the Chichester Arms was built. The Chichester Arms has changed on the outside; the attic windows are no longer in evidence and the signage has changed. It was redesigned in the 1960s with a new façade and new windows; a new buffet was created from the dry cleaners' next door. The bar was extended and transformed from the tiny dark room it had once been. The main doors that were once facing the crossroads have gone and the entrances are now either side.

The Cyprus was first advertised by Robert Schwartz in 1885 but could be older, as in 1883, Christopher Mead advertised the Empress Hotel on Chichester Road and it was on the corner of George Potts Street. In August 1899, the executors of John Turnbull submitted plans to rebuild the public house, and in August the following year revised plans were passed; in 1901, it was opened with this beautiful tile work. It now stands on the corner of Stevenson Street, built on three floors. The lower two were for public use, the ground floor having both a bar and two sitting rooms and the upper floor having a sitting room, a news room, a buffet and a billiard room with bar. Little has changed on the outside except the signage but, like most public houses of today, the inside has changed with the times to cater for the modern clientele.

There has been a village at Westoe for over 800 years and it was originally a mile to the south-east of South Shields on the Sunderland Road. A little over 150 years ago, Westoe was still a little country village, so rural that neither the Crown nor the Jolly Mariners opened on a Sunday; on weekdays they were the quietest of places. It was gradually absorbed into the urban sprawl as South Shields grew from a hamlet by the riverside to the town it is today. Westoe had three public houses: the Crown Inn on what was called Westoe Lane, the Three Mariners in the village and the Westoe Tavern.

The Crown Inn was possibly the oldest public house in the village of Westoe, dating back to at least the middle of the 1700s; in 1803 Thomas Temple was the owner. In 1821 Isabella Weatherhead was landlady at the Crown, which stood on the land now occupied by Wyvestow Lodge. John Thompson was the last landlord of the Crown Inn before it reverted back to a house and smithy.

In 1827, James Hopkirk had a board (a public house with no name) at Westoe. By 1834, he had named it the Westoe Tavern. In 1846, William Easton became the owner and by 1850 he was also known as a market gardener. In 1865, his son, George Easton, who was also a farmer at Horsley Hill, took over the tavern, which became known as George Easton's Inn; the Westoe Tavern stayed in the Easton family until 1885. In 1893, Robert Henderson, owner of Westoe Brewery, took over the Westoe Tavern. In 1891, the Westoe Tavern was rebuilt for the widening of the Sunderland Road and in 1895 the name changed to the County Hotel.

Originally called the Jolly Mariners, the Three Mariners enjoyed green lawns to the front, with a white painted post and chain fencing giving it a picturesque look. In 1858, Miss Margaret Alderson, the landlady at the time, changed the name to the Mariner's Arms Inn. Mrs Jane Birch was the last landlady to advertise the Mariners, in Christies' 1871 Directory, before its licence was transferred to the Westoe Hotel.

Planning permission was granted on 4 April 1871 for the building of one house in Westoe Back Lane (Horsley Hill Road); the landlord was given as J. Hinde. In July 1872, plans for new stables were passed, and when plans for alterations were passed on 15 November that year, the owner was given as R. Hodge. William Davidson first advertised the Westoe Hotel in 1875 and it is still open today.

In 1782, 'Jack the Blaster' made the first steps down the cliffs to the cave he had made his home. It was not until fifty years later that Peter Allan Jnr started excavating the rock that was to become his fifteen-room home and started a business there, but it was not until 1873 that Miss Mary Allan advertised the Grotto as a public house. During the First World War, the steps on the rugged ledge were demolished as a precaution against invaders. After the war, a second staircase was built; it contains 119 twisting steps and is a public right of way. Once again, the Marine Grotto was closed because of the war in 1940. The Marine Grotto has changed quite considerably over the last 150 years. A lift, taking forty seconds, has been installed to make the public house more accessible, making the Marine Grotto unique in Britain.

The Marsden Inn has been rebuilt twice in the last 150 years. Originally, it was on the other side of Redwell Lane to its present position, and then rebuilt 100 yards up the road. This photograph shows the Marsden Inn situated where the far end of Grotto Road is now. From the side of the inn, a path ran down toward the Marsden Grotto, possibly where the path through the houses is now, though in those days it went under the railway lines. In 1879, Sidney Miles Hawkes advertised the Marsden Inn for the first time. Like the Marine Grotto, the Marsden Inn would rely on the men working at the quarry or lime kilns nearby, possibly dropping in on their way home, standing on the old flagged floor in front of a roaring fire.

Standing on the corner of Sunderland Road and Moor Lane East, the Vigilant Inn was originally called the Three Horse Shoes; in 1848, Robert Hodgson advertised the inn as the Cross Keys. When it was taken over by smith James Dixon in 1850, he renamed it the Dun Cow Inn. In 1857, Nicholas Brown advertised the public house as the Steam Boat Inn, but the next year, Mrs Isabella Brown named it the Vigilant Inn. Planning permission was granted on 22 March 1923 to rebuild the Vigilant Inn.

On 3 April 1938, Wm. McEwan & Co. was granted planning permission to build a new hotel on the corner of Marsden Road and Redwell Lane, which they again called the Marsden Inn Hotel. Today it is a very well-known landmark, which sits on the busy roundabout that leads down to the beach.

Harton was a village and township in the parish of Jarrow, about 2 miles south-east of South Shields and 1 mile from Westoe Village, which was absorbed into the town of South Shields in 1917.

In 1828, there were two public houses at Harton, the Three Horse Shoes, with David Law as landlord and the Ship, whose landlord was John Rippon.

Built around 1803, the Ship Inn stands on the corner of Marsden Road and Sunderland Road. Having been altered several times, the central door no longer exists. The emblem above the door goes back to when there was a blacksmith shop at the rear of the public house and reads: 'By hammer and hand all art doth stand.' George Petrie had the Ship Inn altered in 1931.

When the West Park Hotel was sold at auction in 1902 for £15,250, it was described as

> a handsomely appointed Hotel, containing two Kitchens, and very large and lofty Cellars in the Basement; on the Ground Floor is a very large Buffet Bar, and Smoke Room, besides Bar and Snug and Wholesale Department, Smoke Room, Dressing Room, Baths, Lavatory, and W.C., excellent Yard, with Bicycle House and usual Out-offices. On the First Floor is an exceptionally large Banquetting (sic) Room, large Billiard Room, Drawing Room, Dining Room, Kitchen, W.C., and Lavatory. On the Second Floor there are nine Bedrooms, Bath Room, Housemaid's Closet, Lavatory and W.C., etc.

The owner at the time was Cllr John Reay. The West Park public house unfortunately closed in 2014.

Built on the corner of Talbot Road in the late 1890s, John Duncan was the manager in 1898. This once-thriving public house was the meeting place of the Shakespeare Lodge of the Loyal Order of Ancient Shepherds, who would meet in the side room. Today, the public house is closed and has been converted into a Tavistock Retro Restaurant.

Margaret Bulmer, a grocer and flour dealer, first advertised the Victoria Inn situated on the corner of Harton Lane and Boldon Lane in 1853. In 1883, John Andrew Winskill had become the landlord and in 1893 the address became Harton Colliery. In 1900, Mary Winskill became the landlady but the public house had retained the Winskill name; the name continued until it closed. In 2013, it was converted into flats.

The Golden Lion was originally called the West Harton Inn by William Jordison, a farmer, in 1850. In 1858, he called the public house the Wheat Sheaf Inn and in 1879 he advertised the inn as the Golden Lion Hotel. In the 1881/82 Directory, William Jordison calls the hotel the Jordison Hotel. It was once known as the 'top house', because it was the last public house before you crossed what was then the boundary. The Golden Lion closed in July 2006 and was pulled down to make way for five flats.

Built as the Colliery Hotel on the corner of Stanley Terrace and Boldon Lane, in 1850 it was advertised for the first time by George Wardle, who was a butcher. On 4 December 1913, W. D. Reid & Co. Ltd. submitted plans to rebuild the Colliery Hotel and, although it has been altered since, it is the only one still open at West Harton today.

akespeare Inn, Bede St. 1937

Originally called the General Havelock Inn, this public house was built on the corner of Bede Street and Frost Street in the 1860s and first advertised by Edward Smith in 1865. In 1871, Thomas Bell renamed the public house the Shakespeare Inn. In 1935, the Shakespeare Inn was altered, with a door put in instead of a window in Bede Street, and the main door, which had been on the corner, was removed. The publican's licence was removed in November 1858 to new premises in Prince Edward Road.

The Dock Hotel, built on the corner of Dock Street and Hudson Street, was first advertised by John Robinson in 1858. I have been told that it had the nickname of the 'Boodie Bar', owing to the ornate green and cream of its exterior tiles. The old Dock Hotel was pulled down to make way for a new housing estate and the New Dock Hotel, which stands on a raised terrace, was opened in June 1964. Alas, it now stands empty, another sign that the young prefer the crowded town public houses.

We have now come full circle and are back to the Grapes Hotel, on the corner of Hudson Street and Slake Terrace.

Acknowledgements

I would like to thank Margaret Hamilton and Pauline Shawyer, who invited me to join them with their project for a display in the old Town Hall, which was on the old hotels, inns and taverns that had been in the town centre of South Shields. Through them I found that several of both my husband's and my ancestors had had taverns in the 1800s. I would also like to thank Margaret, Pauline, Anne Sharp and Pam McTaggart for their kindness and encouragement and for helping me to access a number of photographs for this book.

I would like to thank Catrin Galt of South Tyneside Library for permission to use the photographs from the collections of Amy Flagg, W. Willits, James Henry Cleet and the unknown photographers who have donated their collections to the library. I would also like to thank Julian Harrop of Beamish Museum for giving me access and permission to use photographs from their collection, Garry Wilkinson for photographs and encouragement at the start, Janis Blower of the *Shields Gazette* and Caroline Barnsley for reading the first draft of the manuscript.

I am also grateful to a number of landlords, for allowing internal photographs to be taken of their establishments and for being so helpful. The front cover image is courtesy of Richzena.

Finally, I would like to thank my husband, Colin, for his patience over the three years which I have spent researching all the hotels, inns and taverns of South Shields.

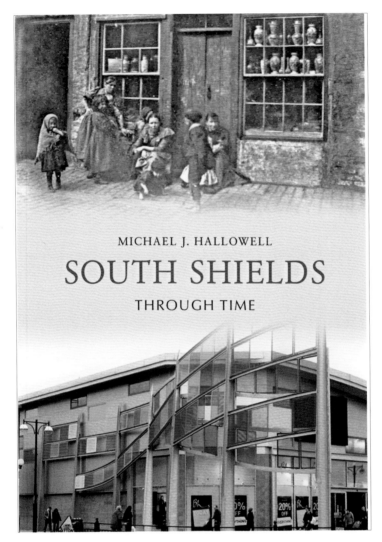

South Shields Through Time

Mike Hallowell

This fascinating selection of photographs traces some of the many ways in which South Shields has changed and developed over the last century.

ISBN 978 1 84868 071 5

96 pages, full colour

Available from all good bookshops or order direct from our website www.amberley-books.com

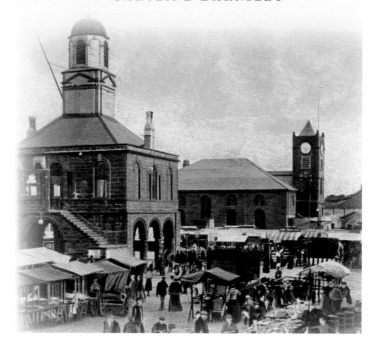

SOUTH SHIELDS

THE POSTCARD COLLECTION

CAROLINE BARNSLEY

South Shields Postcard Collection

Caroline Barnsley

This captivating selection of postcards captures some of the many
ways in which South Shields has been portrayed in pictures through
the past century.

ISBN 978 1 4456 3446 3
96 pages, full colour

Available from all good bookshops or order direct
from our website www.amberley-books.com